Fatima:
A Pilgrim's Company

by
David Baldwin

All booklets are published thanks to the generous support of the members of the Catholic Truth Society

CATHOLIC TRUTH SOCIETY
PUBLISHERS TO THE HOLY SEE

Contents

This book is dedicated to
the inseparable Sacred Heart of Jesus
and Immaculate Heart of Mary
Cor ad Cor loquitur -
Heart speaks unto Heart

Acknowledgements: With grateful thanks to: Donal Foley and Timothy Tindal-Robertson (World Apostolate of Fatima, England and Wales); Lauri Duffy; Nuno Prazeres (Director, World Apostolate of Fatima); Armando Mendes (Proprietor, Hotel Solar da Marta); Sister Sophie of the Congregation of the Alliance of Saint Mary - all who gave valuable insight and information about this very special place.

Picture credits: page 3 © Jorisvo / Shutterstock.com. Pages 11, 15, 32, 34, 61, 79 © Shrine of Fatima. Pages 47 and 63 © David Baldwin. Page 28 cf Wikimedia.

ISBN 978 1 78469 149 3

Foreword

A hundred years ago in 1917, in desolate moorland in the centre of Portugal, Our Lady appeared to three young shepherd children in six apparitions. The messages that she gave them, as God's unlikely messengers, were of such significance as to shape the future history of Portugal, and inform future Church and world events. But also at an individual level, her guidance is not to be resisted - teaching each one of us the value of prayer and sacrifice, and the way that we as Christian people can contribute to our - and others' - salvation.

I warmly welcome this all-encompassing little book on Fatima. It provides sufficient to whet the potential pilgrim's appetite, inform the 'armchair pilgrim', and provide all that is needed for a pilgrimage to Fatima, with background and practical facts, and relevant prayers and meditations to accompany the journey.

The Centenary of 2017 demonstrates most powerfully the relevance of Our Lady of Fatima's messages. By their very durability these messages will continue to resonate. As succinctly put by Portuguese Cardinal Martins, "It is evident that the prophecy of Fatima is not over, and continues to shape the Church and believers".

I wish every blessing to all pilgrims, as they seek the intercession and inspiration of Our Lady of Fatima.

✠ Vincent Cardinal Nichols
Archbishop of Westminster
London, November 2016

Fatima - Introduction

"The sun's disc did not remain immobile. This was not the sparkling of a heavenly body, for it spun round on itself in a mad whirl. Then, suddenly, one heard a clamour, a cry of anguish breaking from all the people. The sun, whirling wildly, seemed to loosen itself from the firmament and advance threateningly upon the earth as if to crush us with its huge and fiery weight. The sensation during those moments was terrible. During the solar phenomenon...there were changes of colour in the atmosphere...I saw everything an amethyst colour. Objects around me, the sky and the atmosphere, were of the same colour...I turned away and shut my eyes, keeping my hands before them to intercept the light. With my back still turned, I opened my eyes and saw that the landscape was the same purple colour as before... All the phenomena which I have described were observed by me in a calm and serene state of mind and without any emotional disturbance." (Eyewitness account of a young lawyer, Dr Jose Almeida Garrett)

This powerful, overwhelming and spectacular solar phenomenon was experienced by an estimated seventy thousand people gathered on 13th October 1917 in the desolate, rural location of Cova da Iria, central Portugal, and attested, as above, by many varied sources. It was the miracle promised by the Virgin Mary to the three young shepherd children to whom she had appeared on five previous occasions that year. It was the miracle that concluded the apparitions of Fatima, the means by which God wished to place his dramatic messages before the people of the world for them to understand and heed, trusting in the simple testimony of three young children - the messengers of God - as so often seen in previous apparition events, such as Lourdes, La Salette and Pontmain.

This Book

This small book tells this story, describing events and personalities, summarising the messages, and giving a narrative description of the pilgrim experience of the Fatima Sanctuary of today. And in so doing, it seeks to inspire your pilgrimage to Fatima, and whilst there, for you to ponder these happenings at source, assisted by appropriate accompanying prayers and meditations, and for you to return home with your experiences and aspirations, and act on them.

It is not a guide book in the conventional sense of giving comprehensive specific details of events, accommodation or travel times - these tend to change and fluctuate over time and season, and this type of information is given in other publications or relevant internet sites. Some major organisations and contacts regarding Fatima are listed at the back of the book.

Fatima Background

Looking round Fatima today, whether from within the Sanctuary or in the town, you would be hard pressed to realise that a short hundred years ago there was very little here in terms of human habitation. It was bare, desolate, undulating moorland, providing just enough rough grazing for sheep. It consisted of scrubby vegetation, littered with unforgiving limestone outcrops and rocks, populated by hardy olive trees and the pervasive holm oak. The area where the Sanctuary now sits was known as Cova da Iria ('valley', or 'hollow of peace'). A few small hamlets were scattered widely, one of which was Aljustrel, two kilometres from Cova da Iria, and central to the Fatima story. A kilometre from Aljustrel was the parish church of Fatima serving this scattered community.

Fatima is located in the centre of Portugal, some 125 kilometres north of Lisbon. It is a civil parish within the municipality of Ourem, and a church parish within the Diocese of Leiria-Fatima. It has a temperate maritime climate - a mixed bag - affected variously by Atlantic, Continental and Mediterranean influences. It can be chilly and wet during the winter months, becoming drier, sunnier and hot from May onwards, declining again from September.

Legend recalls that the Arabic name, Fatima (that of the prophet Mohammed's daughter), was that of a Moorish princess kidnapped by a Portuguese knight during the Moor's occupation of the Iberian Peninsula, and they fell in love and married. She converted to Christianity, taking the name Oureana. A village given as a wedding gift was named after her, which over time was shortened to today's nearby Ourem. She died young, and was buried in monastic grounds not far from Ourem. A small commemorative chapel was built there - the place being named after her - Fatima.

The village of Fatima, with its active parish church, is still very much in evidence, being some two kilometres from the Sanctuary. One can only assume during and immediately after the events of 1917, and the fact they happened in the parish of Fatima, that by default and convenience, the specific area of Cova da Iria became to be referred to as Fatima, which stuck. This strange confluence of a prominent Arabic name with the 'hollow of peace' gives rise to hope of the universality and the reach of Our Lady Queen of Peace, with her influence radiating out from here.

Fatima Today

Today's modern town has approximately eleven thousand souls, many of whom are preoccupied with hosting the four million or so pilgrims that come here every year. Despite those many pilgrim visitors, it is a laid-back, relaxed and pleasant place, with a very Mediterranean feel about it, accentuated by the white-walled, red-tiled houses. These pilgrims come to offer their devotions and intercessions to Our Lady of Fatima, some to marvel at the wonders of the supernatural happenings that occurred here in 1917, and many others to ponder the messages imparted by Our Lady to the *pastorinhos*, the child shepherds. It is one of the best known Catholic pilgrim destinations, and has endured as a beacon of the Church for a century. But for these events, this place would no doubt have remained in total obscurity as history passed it by.

Similarly, three young children from Aljustrel - Lucia Santos, Francisco and Jacinta Marto - may have gone on to anonymous adulthood, striving for their ambitions and dreams of work and family, more than likely staying within the confines of their rural community, had they not been graced by God to receive his Mother, the Blessed Virgin Mary, in a series of six apparitions. Their lives, that of the town, indeed of Portugal, were to change dramatically after that six month period between May and October 1917. And beyond that - the apparitions and messages had ramifications that have echoed round Church history and world events, and continue to do so.

It is a story of many layers. From the initial telling by simple, uneducated children, striving to articulate, be consistent, and having the courage to stand by the incredible supernatural happenings that they had witnessed; to the Church's and the State's reaction; to the response of the people of Portugal; and, in the longer term, of world history. It is a story still underlain with speculation, enigma - and enduring mystery.

Pilgrim Practicalities

Portugal has an excellent road and motorway network (toll paying), and Fatima is very accessible from these. The nearest major airport is Lisbon, to which there are many direct flights from international destinations, including the UK, from where budget airlines also operate.

If flying to Lisbon, the best option to get to Fatima - unless hiring a car - is to catch a coach from Lisbon main coach station (*Sete Rios*) to which you can get either by metro, taxi or shuttle bus from the airport. The coach service is comfortable, regular, well priced and efficient. Train is not recommended, as the nearest station to Fatima is some twenty kilometres away, served by an infrequent local bus service, and no guarantee of taxis being on hand. Parking is free and plentiful round the Sanctuary.

There is a wide selection of hotels and accommodation to suit every depth of pocket. A search through your favourite internet site will indicate these. There is some pilgrim accommodation provided by the Sanctuary for individuals or groups, of which details can be obtained from the Sanctuary's official website.

The Sanctuary on a Fatima Feast Day.

It will be very busy indeed during the major Fatima Feast Days - 13th May and 13th October; Fridays, Saturdays and Sundays during the high season can also be busy, and, when there are any specific rallies or large, visiting pilgrimage groups. There is always a balance to be struck between getting that buzz and inspiration from the presence of large devout crowds, and seeking peace, quiet and tranquillity! Toilet facilities are plentiful around the Sanctuary, and it is very wheelchair friendly.

There are plenty of daily, scheduled Masses and other devotions in the Basilicas and chapels in the Sanctuary, of which the programme is posted prominently at all entrances, in the hotels, and on their website. The winter programme is less extensive than the summer. There is usually an English Mass in the Apparitions Chapel each afternoon at 15:30. Every night there is a candle-lit Rosary procession at 21:30. There are also unadvertised private group Masses and other devotions taking place in the Sanctuary. Visiting groups can arrange their Masses and devotions as advised by the Sanctuary through their website.

A wheeled mini-train rumbles round the Sanctuary, the town and other sites outside the Sanctuary. It is frequent, and provides a hop-on hop-off service.

It is strongly recommended that two days should be an absolute minimum if you want to do full justice to your pilgrimage. There is much to see, take in and contemplate! The Sanctuary website gives details of all aspects.

Lastly, with Fatima being the place of Our Lady of the Rosary, we will maintain our focus on the Rosary by suggesting appropriate decades to be prayed at various places, along with the prayers and meditations. These of course are only suggestions, and are in addition to the full Mysteries that you will pray during your pilgrimage. Complementary to this booklet are two Fatima prayer books published by CTS - *Fatima: Triumph of the Immaculate Heart of Mary Celebrating the First Five Saturdays* and *Fatima's Message and Prayers for Today* (see Bibliography).

Bom Caminho! Have a very blessed pilgrimage!

Blessed those who find their strength in you,
Whose hearts are set on pilgrimage. (*Ps* 84:5)

Events, People and Apparitions

Portugal 1917

Before we look at the events and people directly involved at Fatima, it may be worth taking a brief look at the broader picture in Portugal, which will give some context to the happenings at Fatima.

In 1910 a popular revolution toppled the long established monarchy, and the First Republic was established, where, "The majority of Republicans took the position that Catholicism was the number one enemy… and must be completely broken as a source of influence in Portugal". (Payne, *A History of Spain and Portugal*). In spite of the disastrous economic situation, the new government started devoting its attention to an anti-religious policy. The Catholic Church was targeted straight away: churches were plundered, convents were attacked and clergy were harassed. All residents of religious institutions were expelled and their goods confiscated.

By 1917, the time of the apparitions, with Portugal having entered the First World War without popular consensus, and the revolutionary, reformative policies failing at home, the government was quickly losing "its ability to control events across Portugal… The danger signs were everywhere: urban and rural food riots and assaults on warehouses, the Fatima apparitions and the accompanying clerical mobilisation… the calamitous supply situation of a country that could not feed itself" (*International Encyclopedia of the First World War*). Portugal was in a parlous state.

Despite the active harassment of the Church, there is good reason to believe that this had not permeated significantly to the more isolated, conservative rural areas such as Fatima, where Catholicism was deeply embedded, and was still very much part of the lives of these country folk.

The Children

The Fatima Seers - the three children who witnessed the apparitions - were cousins, all living in the small hamlet of Aljustrel, about two kilometres from the Cova de Iria, where the apparitions took place.

In May 1917, Lucia dos Santos, the eldest, was ten, being the seventh and last child of her family. Being the youngest, she was the family favourite, but despite this, through family need, she started life tending the family flock. She is also noted as being a natural leader, organising prayers, dances and games with the other children in the village.

The other two children were siblings, being the last two of nine. Francisco Marto was nearly nine, and his sister Jacinta, seven. Their parents were devout and God fearing. Francisco was described as being a mild, sensitive boy of

Lucia Santos, Francisco and Jacinta Marto, 1917.

few words - more inclined to think and to listen. Jacinta, in her cousin Lucia's words, "was a child only in years. Her demeanour was always serious and reserved, but friendly."

Looking at photographs of these children, one sees solemn, quite stern faces, radiating an intensity that seems to reflect the enormity of their experiences, and the responsibility they will have felt in consistently conveying the truth of the incredible events they had witnessed.

Whilst their families were poor farming folk, scratching a subsistence living from the land and their animals, they were, as recounted by Lucia in her book, *Fatima in Lucia's Own Words*, generally contented and happy, relying on the bedrock of family support, and their deep faith to sustain them.

Preparatory Apparitions

An apparition is literally an 'appearance', taken from the Latin *apparitio*. It is defined as "a *sensible* manifestation of God, an angel, a saint, or any resurrected soul to a living person (or persons) on earth" (*Encyclopedic Dictionary of Religion*). The word 'sensible' is emphasised here, as the seers respond using their *natural senses*: mainly through physically seeing and hearing with their eyes and ears, talking back and forth, and in some cases touching, smelling, tasting or ingesting: hence the term 'corporeal' - 'bodily'. Thomas listening, talking and then touching Our Lord's wounds is a good example, as is Our Lord breaking and eating bread on the road to Emmaus; in more modern times, the roses and *tilma* of Guadalupe; and, in the context of Fatima, the angel administering the host and chalice to the seers, particularly illustrates this reality. This is distinct from intellectual or imaginative visions which are manifestations of the mind, and not seen physically and externally, such as the mystical experiences described so vividly by St Teresa of Avila.

Whilst Fatima is known principally for the six appearances of Our Lady to the three children in 1917, there were some apparitions prior to these - the precursors - described primarily as the preparation for the central role that Lucia was subsequently to play.

These started in summer 1915, when Lucia, with three other girls from their village, were out tending their sheep. Whilst praying the Rosary after lunch, they became aware of a figure poised above the trees. The figure had no discernible features or substance - as white as snow, but with a transparency, gleaming and dazzling, whilst the sun's rays played around it. The children were transfixed, but continued praying, and on finishing, the figure disappeared. Whilst Lucia told no-one, the other excited children did.

Some short weeks later, on two further occasions, Lucia, accompanied by the same three girls, again saw this gleaming, mysterious, silent figure. Whereas the first account caused more amusement, these further accounts now caused cynicism and some irritation round their village, and Lucia, the darling of the family, suddenly found herself being teased.

How long this situation lasted is not known - it may have just been a transient distraction to the more pressing hardships of daily life. But some short months later, the precursory apparitions were to take on a more profound and specific nature.

The Angel

In the spring of 1916 the three cousins, Lucia, Francisco and Jacinta, were out grazing the sheep at a place called Loca do Cabeco, when they were alerted to a strong wind getting up, shaking the nearby trees. Initially they saw the same indistinct, but radiant figure. But instead of eventually disappearing, it came towards them, and as it drew nearer they clearly saw, "a light, whiter than snow, in the form of a young man, transparent, and brighter than crystal, pierced by the rays of the sun" (*Fatima in Lucia's Own Words*).

The figure came and stood amongst them, saying, "Do not be afraid, I am the Angel of Peace. Pray with me." Then kneeling, with the children following, he touched the ground with his forehead, saying:

> "My God, I believe, I adore, I hope and I love you! I ask pardon of you for those who do not believe, do not adore, do not hope and do not love you!"

He repeated the prayer three times, exhorting the children, “Pray thus. The Hearts of Jesus and Mary are attentive to your supplications”. He then left the children, who stayed repeating the prayer for hours. Francisco, although he saw the angel, did not hear what he said, and had to be told, as was the case for all subsequent apparitions. To forestall a recurrence of the previous teasing, Lucia impressed on them all to keep silent on their return home - which they did.

The second appearance was during the summer of 1916, when the three children were by the well at Lucia’s house. He told them he was the Angel Guardian, the Angel of Portugal, and encouraged them to make sacrifice as reparation for sinners and supplication for conversion, and that by this, they would draw peace down on to Portugal.

The third and last appearance of the angel was the most powerful and most significant, when not only heaven came to earth, but transcended to the children. They were again at Cabeco, praying the angel’s prayer, when they sensed that heavenly light, announcing the presence of the angel. They saw that he held a chalice, above which was suspended a sacred host, from which drops of blood fell into the chalice. The angel knelt before them, leaving the chalice and host suspended. He prayed:

> Most Holy Trinity, Father, Son and Holy Spirit, I adore you profoundly and offer you the most precious Body,

Blood, Soul and Divinity of Jesus Christ present in all the tabernacles of the world, in reparation for the outrages, sacrileges and indifference with which he himself is offended. And through the infinite merits of his most Sacred Heart, and the Immaculate Heart of Mary, I beg of you the conversion of poor sinners.

After the children had repeated this prayer three times he took the host and chalice, placing the host on Lucia's tongue, and administering the chalice to Francisco and Jacinta. The children remained in a state of prayerful ecstasy for many hours, before wearily, but happily returning home. Still they kept silent.

Apparitions of Our Lady

What the expectations of the children were immediately after the angelic apparitions will never be known - for at the time they did not disclose these events at all. It was not until 1937 that Lucia described them in detail in her second memoir, subsequently published in her book *Fatima in Lucia's Own Words*. So, we can only speculate that after the impact had receded with the humdrum events of their lives underway again, that they hugged these extraordinary events closely to themselves. Their demeanour as noted by their families at the time, was one of increased piety, but still behaving and acting quite normally as children. But all this was to change dramatically, and their lives were never to be the same again…

Thirteenth of May 1917

On 13th May 1917, the three cousins herded their flocks to the pasture known as Cova da Iria. After lunch and their customary Rosary, they saw two flashes of what appeared to be lightning, and there, in Lucia's words, "before us on a small holm oak, a lady all dressed in white. She was more brilliant than the sun, and radiated a light more clear and intense than a crystal glass filled with sparkling water, when the rays of the burning sun shine through it".

Lucia recounts that they were not afraid of the lady, but still she reassured them with the first words she spoke: "Do not be afraid, I will do you no harm". Thus reassured, childlike curiosity got the better of Lucia, asking the Lady where she was from ("I am from heaven") and what did she want of them? The response was for them to return to the Cova on the thirteenth day of each month, at the same time, until October. She then said, "Are you willing to offer yourselves to God and bear all the sufferings he wills to send you, as an act of reparation for the conversion of sinners?" Lucia replied, "Yes, we are willing". To which Our Lady said, "Then you are going to have much to suffer, but the grace of God will be your comfort".

At that moment Our Lady opened her hands from which emitted a light so intense, that, "its rays penetrated our hearts and the innermost depths of our souls, making us see ourselves in God who was the light". Her departing words to the children were: "Pray the Rosary every day, in order to obtain peace for the world and the end of the war".

Lucia was naturally reluctant to let anyone know about this encounter, but it was little Jacinta, totally overjoyed by the experience, who excitedly broke the news. The Marto family did not react too unfavourably - there may have been a degree of condescension - but Lucia's mother was very harsh, insisting that she recant. This was the start of much misapprehension, passion and turmoil in these families, in Aljustrel, and in the Church, until it was finally accepted that these children had been chosen by God as his messengers. And in the meantime, it was the children who had to suffer and bear most of this disquiet.

Thirteenth of June 1917

On 13th June the children went to Cova da Iria in anticipation of the midday appearance of Our Lady. About fifty local people also gathered. On her appearance Mary said to Lucia, "I want you to come on the thirteenth of each month; to pray the Rosary every day; and, to learn to read". Lucia then asked her to take them to heaven. Her reply was that Francisco and Jacinta would be taken shortly, but that Lucia would remain on earth to fulfil Jesus's wish to establish a worldwide devotion to her Immaculate Heart. With the same rays of intense light from the first apparition, and, in addition, a heart encircled by piercing thorns displayed in front of Mary's right hand, she departed.

Further trouble ensued from the families - culminating in the children being taken to the parish priest and interviewed. As with every reaction of the Church to this sort of disclosure, he seriously questioned the children, suggesting that they could be suffering some satanic encounter. This threw awful doubt on Lucia, who even contemplated recanting to her mother. She also made her mind up not to go the Cova on 13th July, right up to the last moment, when, "I suddenly felt that I had to go, impelled by a strange force that I could hardly resist".

Thirteenth of July 1917

Word of the apparitions had by now spread, and some three to four thousand people gathered at the Cova. This apparition was the most profound and prophetic of the six. Here Our Lady started with repeating her request for them to come on the 13th of next month, and to pray the Rosary, "to obtain peace for the world, and the end of the war" (World War I). Lucia then asked for a miracle to be worked to dispel any doubts, not only hers, but the rest of the community. The response: "In October I will tell you who I am and what I want, and I will perform a miracle for all to see and believe". Then came one of the central messages, "Sacrifice yourself for sinners and say many times, especially when you make some sacrifice: 'O, Jesus, it is for love of you, for the conversion of sinners, and in reparation for sins committed against the Immaculate Heart of Mary'".

Then came three profound revelations, of which she asked the children to keep secret - the Three Secrets of Fatima.

The first one was a ghastly vision of hell, graphically and subsequently described by Lucia, in which, "Plunged in this fire were demons and souls in human form, like transparent burning embers…floating about in the conflagration…amid shrieks and groans of pain and despair, which horrified us…" Linked to this was the second and prophetic secret that the First World War would end, and: "if people do not cease offending God, a worse one [World War II] will break out during the pontificate of Pius XI", (the identification of this pope was of course not known then).

The third secret was an explicit, visual compilation, depicting the suffering Church over a period of unspecified time - vividly described by Lucia - of which part, "A bishop dressed in white, we had the impression it was the Holy Father, other bishops, priests, men and women religious going up a steep mountain, at the top of which there was a big cross… Before reaching there the Holy Father passed through a big city half in ruins, and half trembling with halting step, afflicted with pain and sorrow, he prayed for the souls of the corpses he met on his way; having reached the top of the mountain, on his knees at the foot of the big cross, he was killed by a group of soldiers who fired bullets and arrows at him, and in the same way there died one after another the other bishops, priest men and women religious, and various lay people of different ranks and positions". These details were not revealed until 2000, at the behest of Pope John Paul II.

To prevent all this, Our Lady asked for the consecration of Russia to the Immaculate Heart of Mary, together with the Communion of Reparation on the First Saturdays, reassuring that whatever the Church would have to endure, "in the end" her Immaculate Heart would triumph. The apparition concluded with Our Lady teaching the children the prayer of forgiveness normally said at the conclusion of each decade of the Rosary: "O my Jesus, forgive us our sins, save us from the fire of hell, and lead all souls to heaven, especially those in most need of your mercy".

Thirteenth of August 1917

By this time news of the apparitions was country wide, including a lot of anti-religious scorn from the secular press. The local Mayor at Ourem was also obviously getting nervous about the local popular religious acclaim, and, in a bid to get on top of the situation and claim kudos for discovering the secrets, kidnapped the seers and took them to his house in Ourem in an attempt to extract the information. They were held over two nights, staying at the Mayor's house, but at one stage being thrown into the communal jail. Despite blandishments, bribes and threats of being boiled alive in olive oil, the children prevailed, refusing to reveal the secret, preferring to face anything rather than disobey Our Lady.

At the Cova da Iria, the thousands who had gathered there heard thunder and saw some flashes of light. A near riot broke out when the news got round that the children had been prevented from coming by the Mayor.

Nineteenth of August 1917

Having missed the encounter on 13th August, one would suppose that the children may then be expecting their next meeting to be 13th September. So, it is probably fair to say that her unannounced appearance whilst they were out grazing at a place called Valinhos on the Sunday after their detention, would have come as a complete and very welcome surprise.

This apparition was relatively short. Our Lady repeated her request for them to continue going to the Cova on the 13th, and to persist in praying the daily Rosary. She also repeated the promise made in July, that in October, "I will perform a miracle so that all may believe", a promise which no doubt gave the children hope and encouragement to stand firm. Before she departed, she said, "Pray, pray very much, and make sacrifices for sinners: for many souls go to hell, because there are none to sacrifice themselves and to pray for them". This exhortation, and the previous vision of hell, urged them to continue offering their own earnest and simple sacrifices like going short on food and water, and spending much time in prayer.

Thirteenth of September 1917

The promise of the October miracle no doubt continued to steady the children, as life at home became even more hectic, with them desperately trying to get on with normality, and avoiding the many curious people seeking them out. So it probably came as some relief when the 13th came round. Despite an estimated thirty thousand people who had gathered at the Cova, they got to the holm oak in time, but not entirely without difficulty, as many wished to entreat or touch the children. Generally though, the crowd were well ordered, many kneeling in prayer and reciting the Rosary.

On appearing, Mary asked the children to continue praying the Rosary to end the war, and reiterated the promise of the miraculous happening for October. Many witnesses testified, including clergy mingling with the crowd, of unnatural phenomena, such as the sky darkening and the stars appearing; a luminous globe moving majestically through the sky from east to west; and, finally a fall of what were described as white petals from the sky which reduced to nothing when they reached the ground.

Thirteenth of October 1917

The waiting and the build up to this day must have been very testing for the children, their families and the local community, as speculation and excitement built. In the days well before mass media, mass transportation, mass accommodation and well developed roads, a staggering seventy thousand people made their way to Cova da Iria to witness the promised miracle. They made their way from all over Portugal, mostly dressed in their Sunday best, arriving in persistent, pouring rain. The national press were there, including the scathing, anti-religious papers, such as *O Seculo*, who had invited people to turn up and mock a 'non-event'.

Somehow the children managed to reach the holm oak tree in time. With the expected flash of light announcing her appearance, Mary again started by making her customary appeal to pray the Rosary, confirming specifically who she was: "I am the Lady of the Rosary". She again predicted

Miracle of the sun.

the impending end of the war, and requested that a chapel be built here in her honour. She concluded sadly, "Do not offend the Lord Our God any more, because he is already so much offended". She then rose towards the east, projecting the bright rays.

At this point Lucia involuntarily cried out, "Look at the sun!": the clouds cleared, the rain stopped, and the sun started moving dramatically about the sky, seeming to whirl and plunge terrifyingly earthward, projecting a beautiful, vivid coloured light of blue, yellow and purple. There are many consistent accounts of this phenomenon, with some people focusing on different aspects.

Collective religious hallucination and hysteria has been ruled out, as many people some kilometres away, and not connected to the event, also witnessed it; as was confirmation by meteorologists and astronomers that there was no unusual solar activity detected that day. The anti-secular press could but only report objectively what they saw:

> But at that moment a great shout went up and one could hear the spectators nearest at hand shouting: "A miracle! A miracle!" Before the astonished eyes of the crowd, whose aspect was biblical as they stood bareheaded, eagerly searching the sky, the sun trembled, made sudden incredible movements outside all cosmic laws - the sun "danced" according to the typical expression of the people. (*O Seculo*)

Whilst this was occurring, the children alone saw the appearances, as promised previously by Our Lady, of St Joseph, holding the Child Jesus with Mary; followed by Jesus and Mary, appearing as Our Lady of Sorrows; and, finally Mary as Our Lady of Mount Carmel, clearly displaying the brown scapular, all respectively mirroring the Rosary theme: the Joyful, Sorrowful and Glorious Mysteries.

When all this spectacular activity, estimated at about ten minutes, had ceased, everyone suddenly noticed, with wonder, that their sodden clothes and the slushy, muddy ground were all now completely dry.

After this day, once again the lives of the children, the local community, and indeed Portugal, were to change dramatically, as well as the subsequent unfolding of world events as foretold in the apparitions.

The Sanctuary

What may immediately strike you, from whatever point you enter the Sanctuary, is the sheer size of the concourse or *Recinto* - stretching away - rising at each end and dipping in the centre. Your eye may then be drawn to the elegant, pale stone Basilica at one end, with its tiered tower reaching skyward, topped with a crown and cross, and its extensive, handsome arcing colonnades reaching out from each side of the church, embracing the concourse. This is the Basilica of Our Lady of the Rosary.

Ironically, the raison d'etre of Fatima may not immediately catch your attention as you continue to scan the area - the Chapel of Apparitions (*Capelinha*), built over the place where the apparitions occurred, and which is enclosed by the low, flat-roofed, glass-sided, inconspicuous building close to, and below the Basilica, standing next to a large, green tree, and with immediately in front, a gold statue of the Sacred Heart of Jesus atop a short column.

This is one reason why my preference on arriving at a site like this, after an initial scan round, is to take a gentle stroll without getting into any detail, just to identify the separate elements and start to fit them in together, forming first impressions, and getting a feel for the place.

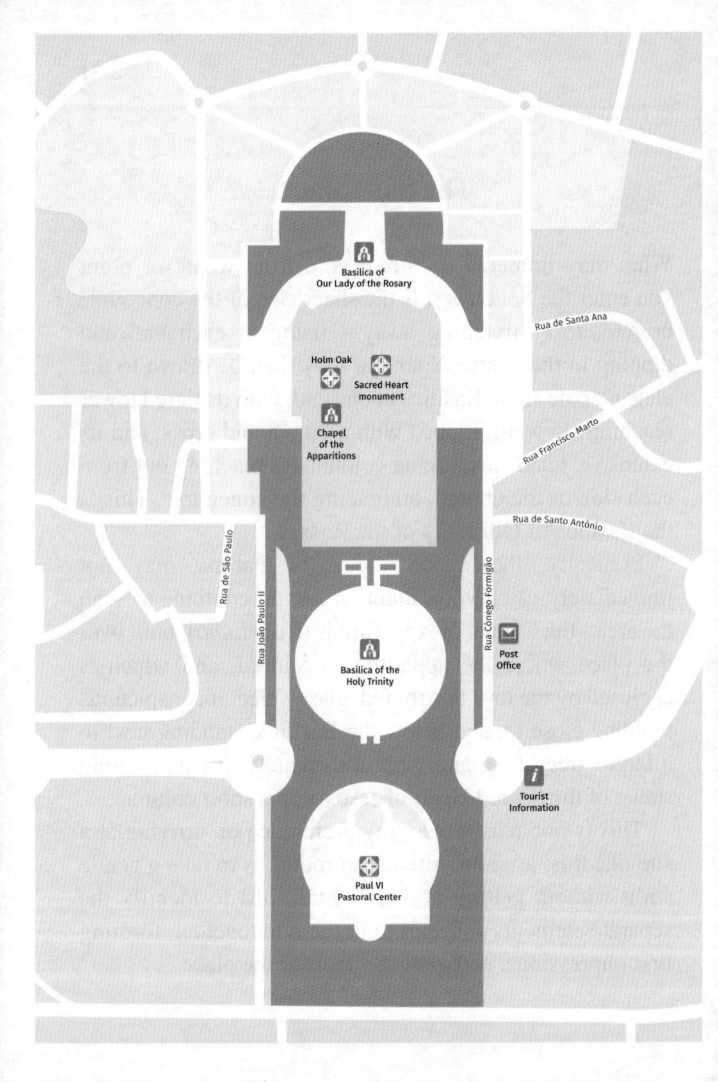
Basilica of
Our Lady of the Rosary
Rua de Santa Ana
Holm Oak
Sacred Heart
monument
Chapel
of the
Apparitions
Rua Francisco Marto
Rua de Santo António
Rua de São Paulo
Rua João Paulo II
Rua Cônego Formigão
Post
Office
Basilica of the
Holy Trinity
Tourist
Information
Paul VI
Pastoral Center

Close to the Chapel of Apparitions you may notice a column of rising smoke which comes from the votive candle gallery, and not far from that, the helpful Information Office. Heading up the gentle slope of the concourse you will see the narrow marble strip of the penitential pathway leading up towards a sizeable, low, flat-topped, pale stone circular building - the new Basilica of the Most Holy Trinity. To the left of that Basilica, the distinctive, modernistic High Cross. In the flat plaza fronting the Basilica, are stairs leading down to an underground 'street', the Galilee of St Peter and St Paul, containing various chapels and spaces, all to which we will return in more detail.

Strolling back down towards the Rosary Basilica you will see that the concourse is flanked by other more functional buildings - administrative offices, and some pilgrim accommodation. Most of the concourse is tree lined and pleasantly shaded, with long stone benches on which to rest. Although the Sanctuary sits right in the middle of the town, it is not crowded by the town, whilst still allowing convenient access to both.

Chapel of Apparitions

"In the light of the mystery of Mary's spiritual motherhood, let us seek to understand the extraordinary message, which began on 13th May 1917 to resound throughout the world from Fatima."

(St John Paul II, Homily at Fatima, 13th May 1982)

Foreground - Chapel of Apparitions and statue of the Sacred Heart.
Background - Basilica of the Holy Rosary.

Where you decide to head for next and start immersing yourself, is of course entirely your choice - my strong desire was to head for the *Capelinha*. The dip in which the chapel sits still gives that feeling of being in that 'hollow of peace' - the Cova da Iria. The distinctive, iconic statue of Our Lady of Fatima inside the *Capelhina* marks the exact location of the apparitions where she appeared above a small holm oak tree. This is where, on that rough, empty pasture land, the first small chapel was erected in 1919 in compliance with Our Lady's request during the apparitions, "I want you to build a chapel here in my honour", as well as marking the place and providing the focus for the many pilgrims who were now coming to the Cova da Iria. It was blown up in 1922 by anti-religious elements, and promptly rebuilt that year.

In 1982 the current glass-sided and open-ended chapel was built, enclosing the (refurbished) original chapel. It is usually a place of quiet contemplation, reflection and prayer, where the intense devotion being displayed is palpable, but you have to choose your times, as Masses and Rosaries are often underway, in many languages. Simple, sturdy, low wooden benches are ranged on three sides, looking up to a small altar, behind which is the statue and the original chapel.

The statue of Our Lady of Fatima is of Brazilian cedar, carved in 1920. It was crowned by the Papal Legate, Cardinal Masella, on behalf of Pope Pius XII, on 13th May 1946, with the precious crown of gold and jewels, all donated by the women of Portugal. The crown is beautifully displayed in the Sanctuary Museum, and is only placed on the statue for the International Mass on the 13th of the month and major pilgrimage days, and has only left the Sanctuary on nine occasions.

Meditation:
The Sacred and Immaculate Hearts

Do you fear to slight the incomparable goodness of the Heart of Jesus, your God and Redeemer, if you invoke the charity of his Mother's Heart? Do you not know that Mary is nothing, possesses nothing and can do nothing except in, through and by Jesus? Do you not know that Jesus is everything and that he can and does accomplish everything through her? Do you not know Jesus made Mary's Heart as it is, and that he willed it to be the fountain of light, of consolation, and of every possible grace for those who will have recourse to it in their necessities? Do you forget that not only does Jesus reside and dwell perpetually in Mary's Heart, but that he is in truth the Heart of her Heart and the soul of her soul; and that therefore coming to the Heart of Mary means to honour Jesus, and to invoke her Heart is to invoke Jesus? (St John Eudes)

Prayer:

Consecration to the Immaculate Heart of Mary

(from the Sanctuary prayer card)

Virgin Mary, Mother of God and our Mother, to your Immaculate Heart we consecrate ourselves, in an act of total entrustment to the Lord.

By you we will be led to Christ. By him and with him we will be led to the Father.

We will walk in the light of faith, and we will do everything so that the world may believe that Jesus Christ is the one sent by the Father.

With him we wish to carry his love and salvation to the ends of the earth.

Under the protection of your Immaculate Heart, we will be one people with Christ. We will be witnesses of his Resurrection. By him we will be led to the Father, for the glory of the most Holy Trinity, whom we adore, praise and bless forever. Amen.

When we enter the communion of life with Mary, through self entrustment to her, we also start on the path of fuller growth of unity with Jesus - on the path to holiness. (Fr Tadeusz Dajczer)

Rosary: *The Birth of Jesus*

(third decade of the Joyful Mysteries)

Basilica of Our Lady of the Rosary

"Mary is never far from us when we pray the Rosary, for when we call upon her while meditating on Mysteries of the Rosary, we see Christ through her eyes, and thus do we really come to know him."
("Marian Meditation and Prayer", Bishop William E Lori)

This graceful, gleaming neo-classical church sits majestically at the north eastern end of the Sanctuary. One cannot help but admire and marvel at this elegant structure, not only rising skyward, but embracing the Sanctuary with its wide-reaching, classical colonnades, welcoming the pilgrim with open arms to climb the wide steps beneath, and enter the church. On the steps in front is the altar and canopy for the outdoor Masses.

The Basilica was built over the area where the *pastorhinos*, the child shepherds, used to play whilst tending their sheep. Construction, from local limestone, began in 1928, and it was consecrated in 1953. The tower reaches sixty five metres high, surmounted by the prominent gilded crown, with cross on top - seen from afar when illuminated at night. The carillon consists of sixty two bells, being heard when the tuneful '*Aves*' are rung out every hour.

The prominent statue of the Immaculate Heart of Mary above the entrance porch bids you welcome. It is a gift from the people of the USA, and was carved from a single block of Carrara marble by an American priest, Fr Thomas McGlynn. He worked closely with Sr Lucia in the initial stages of design, verifying the likeness of Our Lady of Fatima. It was blessed by Pope Pius XII.

When you enter the Basilica, and once your eyes have adjusted, you get an immediate impression of light, length and loft, as your eye travels down the long, single nave to the altar and apse above, and then up to the gold arch, and to the simple, white barrelled ceiling, pierced along both sides by clerestory stained glass windows. The whole interior is mainly shining white and cream, lit by the triple layer of many stained glass windows.

As you walk down the nave, past the solid, dark pews, you will notice the seven arched side chapels on each side. Each represents, in sequence, a decade of the Mysteries of the Rosary, being portrayed above each altar by a striking bas-relief of gilded bronze, with a stained-glass semi-circular window of the Litany of Our Lady. The fifteenth decade is the last of the Glorious Mysteries, the Coronation of Our Lady, displayed by the prominent bas-relief in the apse, high above in the sanctuary.

You will now have reached the transept, the construction of which was gifted from the people of Great Britain and Ireland. On the left are the tombs of Blessed Jacinta and Sr Lucia: simple floor-level marble slabs with their names engraved. Above, is a polychrome statue of Jacinta, holding a lamb. People will be gathered round, focusing intently. A time of reflection here, as you ponder these two close childhood friends, and the central role they played in the tumultuous events of Fatima, and now, rejoicing in their glorious heavenly reunion.

In the opposite side transept, lies Blessed Francisco, the young, pensive lad, Jacinta's brother. Above his tomb is a bronze statue of him, again holding a lamb; and on the tomb, two birds, reflecting his love of nature. More time for reflection for this prayerful boy, who although did not hear, saw all, understood all. The remains of Jacinta were interred in 1951, and Francisco's in 1952. Sr Lucia was buried here in 2006.

As you now turn your attention to the sanctuary, you will take in the small, modern, bronze altar at the front, used for the routine celebration of Mass; and the high altar at the back in delicate pink marble, on which sits the silver tabernacle. The statue of Our Lady of Fatima by the communion rail on the right is the first of the 'Virgin Pilgrim' statues that started worldwide travels in 1947. The painting above the altar depicts Our Lady coming in peace and light, joining the seers, the Church, and the angel with the Eucharist. It also shows the dome of St Peter's in Rome, and the popes closely associated with Fatima - John Paul II, John XXIII and Paul VI, emphasising this unique aspect of the papal involvement in Fatima.

Finally, high up in the apse, is the bas-relief of the Coronation of Our Lady, all in glowing white. Embracing the sanctuary from above is the golden arch, with the words "*Regina Sacratissimi Rosarii Fatimae Ora Pro Nobis*" - Queen of the Most Holy Rosary of Fatima Pray For Us.

Meditation: *The Rosary*

The Rosary is a simple form of prayer that can be prayed by the young or old, the learned or the uneducated, the saint or the sinner. Each can adapt it to his or her own capacity. It is so pleasing to Our Lady, because it brings us to review again and again the life of Christ, the mysteries of our redemption.

After repeatedly asking for the daily Rosary, and identifying herself as "the Lady of the Rosary", the Blessed Mother terminated the final apparition by showing the children three separate tableaux symbolising the entire message of the Rosary. The first was a vision of the Holy Family - representing the Joyful Mysteries; the second a vision of Our Lady of Sorrows - representing the Sorrowful Mysteries; and the third a vision of Our Lady of Mount Carmel - representing the Glorious Mysteries.

The Rosary may seem like an insignificant thing in the light of the magnitude of the evils of today's world, but it is the weapon given to us by Our Lady. She merely asks our co-operation, and she will do the rest. It is like the slingshot of David that killed the mighty enemy because the power of God was behind it. Thus, as the saying goes, "They who pray the Rosary have the power of God in their hands". (The Rosary Confraternity)

***Prayer:** Dedicated to Our Lady of the Rosary*
(composed by Pope Francis)

We entrust our miseries, the many streets of hate and blood, the thousands of ancient and new poverties, and above all, our sins. To you we entrust ourselves, Mother of Mercy: grant us the forgiveness of God to help us to build a world according to your Heart. O Blessed Rosary of Mary, sweet chain that ties us to God, chain of love that makes us brothers and sisters, we will not leave you again. You will be in our hands a weapon of peace and forgiveness, a star that guides our path.

***Rosary:** The Coronation of Our Lady as Queen of Heaven and Earth*
(fifth decade of the Glorious Mysteries)

Outside

When you exit the church you will notice the Stations of the Cross, strikingly depicted in polychrome on ceramic tiles, set back in the arched recesses of the colonnades each side of the church. The colonnades continue symmetrically to link up with other buildings on either side of the *Recinto*.

As you move further away, and looking up at the church, you will notice the statues on top of the colonnades. The four larger statues closer to the church are Portuguese saints; the remainder are French, Italian, Spanish, and one English (the Carmelite, St Simon Stock). There are eighteen statues in total, although the more observant may only count seventeen obvious shapes - the statue of St John Bosco is sculpted standing together with his pupil, St Dominic Savio.

Between the Basilica and the *Capelinha* is a large, well protected holm oak tree, under which the children sheltered, praying the Rosary, whilst awaiting the appearance of Our Lady. The small holm oak, over which Our Lady appeared, and marked by the position of the statue in the *Capelinha*, was pulled apart by pilgrims after the apparitions, never to recover.

Just opposite the *Capelinha*, in the centre of the *Recinto* is the gilded bronze statue of the Sacred Heart of Jesus. It was the gift of a pilgrim, and blessed in position in 1932. A spring of water was unearthed whilst excavations were being made here, which was unusual for this area where artesian wells are very rare. There are taps round the base of the statue for pilgrims to draw water.

Votive candles of all sizes for the nearby candle gallery can be bought from the stand behind it, or from many shops in town. The helpful Sanctuary Information Office is also nearby.

Almost opposite the Sacred Heart statue, against a wall on the other side from the *Capelinha*, near one of the exits, is the modern, abstract, triangular metal sculpture depicting the Nativity.

Sanctuary Museum

The Museum is housed in the building just past the Nativity sculpture, entering through the door marked *Luz e Paz* - which is the title of the display: "Light and Peace". The whole is a very tasteful presentation of the Fatima story. There is an initial dramatic entry through a dark corridor with a First World War theme, through which you have a temporary feeling of being lost. From there you will enter a small cinema room, where the events of Fatima are screened, with accompanying commentary. Through a curtain on the left of the cinema room you then enter the series of display rooms.

These varied displays present a host of Fatima related objects. The first and most striking is the glittering, fabulous gold and bejewelled crown of Our Lady of Fatima, weighing 1.2 kilos, encrusted with 313 pearls and 2,679 precious stones. Clearly visible, mounted on the underside of the blue encrusted globe at the top of the crown, is one of the bullets fired in the assassination attempt on St John Paul II. With the crown is the papal ring placed at the foot of the statue in the *Capelinha* by St John Paul II in 2000, "as a sign of my profound gratitude for the protection she has afforded me". This ring was presented to him by the heroic Cardinal Stefan Wyszynski, the defender of the Church in Poland against communism.

The ensuing showcases present many liturgical and other precious objects, one of the most striking being the magnificent Irish monstrance, forty two inches high and weighing seventeen pounds. It is of silver and gold, mounted with about 1,700 precious jewels in a most intricate design, being a gift from the Irish people. Another item of interest is the English chalice presented in thanksgiving for the cessation of the bombing of the London Blitz, following prayers offered at Fatima by the women of Portugal.

As you move through, you will see frame upon frame of delicately and thematically arranged precious gold and jewellery items presented in thanksgiving by individuals; sports items given by famous sportspeople, others representing the many trades and professions; papal, liturgical, baptismal, wedding garments and other personal objects. There is a map of the world showing where the Virgin Pilgrim statue has travelled since 1947, and many intriguing objects and items from various countries associated with her travels. Towards the end there is a Golden Rose, that most special pontifical gift, given to people and places of rare distinction, on this occasion by Pope Paul VI, and a second one presented by Pope Benedict XVI in 2010. The final section is dedicated to St John Paul II, and objects donated by him.

You can either opt to accompany an English speaking guide on a tour of the museum, for which you will have to check the time, and book, or you can self conduct, with the very adequate booklet provided on entry, taking a chance on when the film is screened and in what language.

Also, as you enter this building, on the left is an office where you can purchase a stipend, currently ten euros, for Mass to be celebrated in the *Capelhina* for your intentions.

Berlin Wall

As you leave the museum, turning left and walking on past the building, you will come to some steps on your left going up out of the Sanctuary. Going up them, you will see under some trees on the left, a full-height segment of the Berlin Wall in a glass encased shelter. This was presented by the Portuguese emigrants in Germany in thanksgiving for the fall of communism, as promised at Fatima, and brought about by St John Paul II's act of consecration of 25th March 1984.

From here, continuing on up the slope you will soon be at the Basilica at the opposite end of the Sanctuary - the Most Holy Trinity. It was built to accommodate the ever growing numbers of pilgrims to Fatima. It is set in an extensive and attractive area of patterned cobblestones. Immediately by the Basilica is the large, dramatic, modernistic High Cross, and placed at all four 'corners', celebrating the popes who have strong associations with Fatima, are statues of St John Paul II, Pius XII ('the Pope of Fatima'), Paul VI and Bishop Jose de Silva (Bishop of Leiria-Fatima from 1920-1957).

Basilica of the Most Holy Trinity.

The Basilica of the Most Holy Trinity

The Paraclete, the Holy Spirit, whom the Father will send in my name, will teach you everything and remind you of all I have said to you. (*Jn* 14:26)

The Basilica itself is circular, low silhouetted - plain and unassuming from the outside. Part of the architect's brief was to design a building that could accommodate over eight thousand worshippers, but not dominate and distract from the rest of the Sanctuary - this is the perfect solution. Construction started in 2004, and the completed church was consecrated in 2007.

You are drawn in to enter through the two stark, substantial concrete arms reaching out into the plaza from the entrance porch. The porch's rear walls present attractive plaques depicting the Mysteries of the Rosary, and expansive glass designs of Bible quotations in six languages. You enter through the massive eight metre high bronze doors - dedicated to Christ. There are another twelve of these doors placed round the Basilica, each dedicated to an apostle (Matthias in place of Judas Iscariot).

On entering you cannot help but be impressed by the size and clean lines of this simple church, the shining, pale marble floor gently sloping from rear to front, and without any obstructing pillars, allowing all worshippers a clear view of the raised altar.

You will immediately catch the brilliant, vibrant gold mosaic in the apse - by Slovenian priest, Fr Marko Rupnik - stretching nearly the full width of the church, and the dramatic, powerful, bronze crucifix - by the Irish sculptor Catherine Greene - immediately above the altar. There is space for one hundred celebrants behind the altar.

Apart from the one statue by the altar, the remainder of the church is in the style of a liturgical church - plain and entirely devoid of distraction from other statues, stained glass windows and other ornamentation so often seen and expected in our devotional churches. The central and side naves are generous, allowing room for many people to circulate, and the light, solid wood pews are comfortably padded to sit and kneel on.

On moving down the central nave you will start noticing the detail of the mosaic - themed 'the Heavenly

Jerusalem', the Lamb of God behind the crucifix, and to the left as you view, Our Lady, with Jacinta and Francisco in front of her, and just behind, Sr Lucia. The statue on the altar plinth is the Immaculate Heart of Mary, in a graceful gesture of peace and welcome, holding aloft her rosary.

Part of the minimalist appeal of this church is that it is lit from above entirely by natural light through the roof, filtering through the translucent blinds lining the whole ceiling - producing dramatic changes and levels of light when the clouds are moving across the sun.

Participating in Mass here, in a full church, with divine singing and music, is a powerful, moving and inspiring experience.

Meditation: *Unity and Trinity*

There is, however Unity and Trinity; and it was and is and will be forever: understood and adored by faith; through faith, and not through inquiry nor investigation nor demonstration. For as much as you seek, so much the more ignorant will you be; and as much as you pry into it, so much the more will it be hidden. Let God, therefore, be adored by the faithful without meddlesome calculation. Believe that God is in three Persons. How this is, is beyond explaining; for God is not to be comprehended.
(St John Damascene)

Prayer: *Act of Reparation to the Holy Trinity*
(the angel's prayer)

Most Holy Trinity, Father, Son and Holy Spirit, I adore you profoundly and I offer you the most precious Body, Blood, Soul and Divinity of Jesus Christ, present in all the tabernacles of the world, in reparation for the outrages, sacrileges and indifference with which he himself is offended. And through the infinite merits of his most Sacred Heart, and the Immaculate Heart of Mary, I beg of you the conversion of poor sinners.

Rosary: *The Descent of the Holy Spirit on the Apostles and Our Lady*
(third decade of the Glorious Mysteries)

Galilee of Ss Peter and Paul

Immediately in front of the church are steps descending underground (wheelchair ramps at either side of the church). This goes to the 'underground street' or Galilee, meaning entrance area. Various chapels and other spaces are located here. Three of the chapels are primarily dedicated to the Sacrament of Reconciliation - the Sacred Heart, the Immaculate Heart and the Resurrection - which usually takes place between 07:30-13:00 and 14:00-19:30, with digital displays indicating the availability of confessionals and languages of the confessor. The largest chapel - the Death of Jesus - is often used as a Mass venue.

On the other side of the Galilee passageway are decorative water features, a large space for seasonal or themed displays and toilets.

The Chapel of the Blessed Sacrament at one end, is reserved for adoration - which is available during all the opening hours of the Sanctuary. It is a quiet, unadorned space in which Jesus in the Blessed Sacrament is the focus, exposed in a large, unfussy, backlit silver panel, giving the perfect opportunity to engage in some quiet prayer and reflection, away from the bustle of the main Sanctuary.

Meditation: *"...my living God..."*

My heart is drawn here where my God is hidden,
Where he dwells with us day and night.
Clothed in the white host;
He governs the whole world,
he communes with souls.
My heart is drawn here where my God is hiding,
Where his love is immolated.
But my heart senses that the living water is here;
It is my living God, though a veil hides him.
(St Faustina)

Prayer: *To the Sacred Heart of Jesus*
(St Margaret Mary Alacoque)

Lord Jesus,
Let my heart never rest until it finds you,
Who are its centre, its love and its happiness.
By the wound in your Heart
Pardon the sins that I have committed
Whether out of malice or out of evil desires.
Place my weak heart in your own divine Heart,
Continually under your protection and guidance,
So that I may persevere in doing good
And in fleeing evil until my last breath. Amen.

Lucia wrote they were "moved by an interior impulse" to start saying this prayer as the first apparition ended: "O Most Holy Trinity, I adore you! My God, my God, I love you in the most Blessed Sacrament."

Rosary: *The Institution of the Eucharist*
(fifth decade of the Luminous Mysteries)

Behind the Basilica of the Most Holy Trinity is the substantial Paul VI Pastoral Centre, which started construction in 1979, and was blessed by St John Paul II in 1982. It is well equipped with a large amphitheatre to stage major conferences, as well as other, smaller venues to host meetings, reunions and gatherings.

Standing on the plaza by the Basilica of the Most Holy Trinity, you have a good all-encompassing view of the Sanctuary below you. On the left, the buildings linking with the colonnades provide principally, the Retreat House and pilgrim accommodation of Our Lady of Sorrows, and which, at the end of the colonnade at ground level, is the first aid post. On the right is the Retreat House and pilgrim accommodation of Our Lady of Mount Carmel, as well as Shrine administrative offices. Just at the end of this colonnade at first floor level is the small Chapel of the Angel, usually used for small group Masses.

Also, from this viewpoint, over on the left, you may see some pilgrims making their slow, prayerful way on their knees down the Penitential Way to the *Capelinha*. This particular aspect of Fatima came about, when in about 1920, Sister Lucia's mother seemed to be dying, and her sisters blamed Lucia for this, who she said she would entreat Our Lady to cure her. For nine successive days Lucia prayed the Rosary moving on her knees over the rough ground from the road to the site of the apparitions. Through her prayer and penance her mother recovered - but even then she did not believe in the apparitions!

Just beyond the Way you will see the smoke rising up with the prayers of those at the candle stands; in and round the *Capelhina* you will hear the sounds of praying and singing also ascending; and, in the distance, at the far end, you will see pilgrims climbing the steps to enter the

Basilica of the Rosary; you will hear the carillon ringing out the '*Aves*' from the tower... all the sounds and sights of the faithful - praying, seeking, hoping, trusting.

May the God of hope fill you with all joy and peace in your faith, so that in the power of the Holy Spirit you may be rich in hope. (*Rm* 15:13)

Outside the Sanctuary

By contrast to the town-enclosed Sanctuary, there are devotional areas and other places of interest set in peaceful country surroundings just outside Fatima, and are just as much part of your pilgrimage. These are the Way of the Cross; Valinhos, where the fourth apparition of Our Lady took place; Cabeco, the place of the first and third apparitions of the angel; the seers' village of Aljustrel; and, the parish church of Fatima. If you have the time and energy, they are all linked and walkable from the Sanctuary, the furthest being Aljustrel and the Fatima church, both two kilometres from the Sanctuary. The Way of the Cross is just over a kilometre long, located in between the town outskirts and Aljustrel. Alternatively, you can hire a taxi or take the mini-train to drop off and/or pick up points of your choice.

Way of the Cross

The Way of the Cross (*Sacra Via*) consists of fifteen Stations, finishing at the Hungarian Calvary. Fourteen are the gift of Hungarian refugees in the West, with the fifteenth, the Resurrection, being gifted by a Hungarian parish in gratitude for the 'resurrection' of Hungary from the 'communist tomb'. Each Station is beautifully presented in small be-columned, stone chapels, each event being depicted by bas-relief carvings on stone. There are toilet facilities between the ninth and tenth Stations, and at the Hungarian Calvary.

The Way meanders through this peaceful countryside, surrounded by mainly ancient olive trees, the limestone rock and outcrops, with dry-stone walling much in evidence. It is a serene and peaceful experience, walking and praying the Way, listening to the bird song and the gentle soughing of the wind through the trees. Occasionally you may come across organised groups, singing or praying as they progress.

The start of the Way is just off the large Sul roundabout (*Rotunda Sul*); be aware that the first Station is only about a hundred metres down on the left, set back in a laurel hedge niche - I initially missed it in my haste! In between the Stations, and on up the route to and at Aljustrel, you may notice numbered, stone plaques with some text on them - these are quotes in Portuguese from Sr Lucia's Memoirs.

Customary Prayers at Each Station

Before each reflection/prayer:

V. We adore you O Christ and praise you.

R. Because by your Holy Cross you have redeemed the world.

At the end of each reflection/prayer:

I love you, Jesus, my love above all things; I repent with my whole heart for having offended you. Never permit me

to separate myself from you again. Grant that I may love you always; and then do with me what you will.
Our Father… Hail Mary… Glory be…

Valinhos

Some way further along, between two of the Stations, is the area of Valinhos, where Our Lady appeared to the children in the fourth apparition on 19th August, with them not being able to make the Cova da Iria on the 13th, having been kidnapped by the Mayor of Ourem.

A statue of Our Lady, enclosed in a colonnaded and arched edifice, looks prayerfully down. It was here that she told the children to: "Pray, pray very much, and make sacrifices for sinners: for many souls go to hell, because there are none to sacrifice themselves and to pray for them".

Calvary

Past Valinhos, after the tenth Station, the path splits, one route signposted '*Loca da Anjo*', this is the sign for Cabeco, the place of the angel apparitions. Resist the temptation to follow this for the moment, and stay with the signposted Way, until you reach the end at the magnificent and dramatic Calvary group of statues sitting on top of the small, beautifully proportioned Chapel of St Stephen. The chapel has vibrant, miniature stained glass windows, and the ceiling above the nave is a beautifully detailed mosaic of Our Lady of Fatima. Here you can reflect and pray, and contemplate the Calvary scene above.

Meditation: Christ Crucified

Our Lord Jesus is on the cross. His whole body is covered with wounds, his hands and feet are nailed to the cross; his head is crowned with thorns; for his drink, only vinegar and bitter gall. Although he suffered so much, he knows that many will remain indifferent. This mental anguish is even more painful than his physical torment.

God suffered so much for me. Why am I not willing to give up some worldly pleasure and accept some suffering in this life? I know well that Jesus suffered in reparation for my sins and yet I still go against his will and commit sin. How can I reject his grace and increase his sorrow?

Because Jesus suffered in order to save all classes of people, so he accepted sufferings caused by all kinds of people, including all of us. Are we not increasing his suffering by our lack of faith, committing sin and not loving his Sacred Heart?

Where was our Blessed Mother at that time? She was weeping beside the cross, watching her Son suffer. This was not just the human love between mother and son. She united her love of Jesus with her love for all mankind, offering it in sacrifice to God the Father for the salvation of the whole world. Our Lady is indeed the Mother of our salvation.

Each and every one of us should imitate Our Blessed Lady, contemplating Jesus on the cross. We should offer our sufferings in reparation for our sins and those of others, asking for mercy and forgiveness and not fail to respond to the graces Jesus obtained for us through his Passion.

(Cardinal Ignatius Kung - composed during a thirty-year imprisonment and smuggled out of prison and China)

Prayer: *Before a Crucifix*

Behold, O kind and most sweet Jesus, before thy face I humbly kneel, and with the most fervent desire of soul, I pray and beseech thee to impress upon my heart lively sentiments of faith, hope and charity, true contrition for my sins and a firm purpose of amendment. With deep affection and grief of soul, I ponder within myself, mentally contemplating thy five wounds, having before my eyes the words which David the Prophet spoke concerning thee: "They have pierced my hands and my feet, they have numbered all my bones".

On recitation a partial indulgence is granted.

Rosary: *The Crucifixion*

(fifth decade of the Sorrowful Mysteries)

Just beside the Calvary is the fifteenth Station - the Resurrection, at which you can rejoice, before retracing your steps for a short distance and taking the path to Cabeco (*Loca da Anjo*).

Cabeco

This is a sublime and poignant place. It is in amongst woods of ancient and gnarled olive trees, where the first and third apparitions of the angel took place - the third being depicted here by white marble statues. They show the angel devoutly holding the host and chalice, with the children kneeling, hands together, heads bowed in deep reverential prayer, before receiving the host and chalice - for it was here that these children received the Body and Blood of Our Lord from the angel.

On another occasion at Cabeco, Jacinta had a vision of fields full of dead people, others crying from hunger, and the Pope praying to the Immaculate Heart of Mary in a church.

My God, I believe, I adore, I hope and I love you! I ask pardon of you for those who do not believe, do not adore, do not hope and do not love you!

Most Holy Trinity, Father, Son and Holy Spirit, I adore you profoundly and offer you the most precious Body, Blood, Soul and Divinity of Jesus Christ present in all the tabernacles of the world, in reparation for the outrages, sacrileges and indifference with which he himself is offended. And through the infinite merits of

The third Angel apparition, Cabeco.

his most Sacred Heart, and the Immaculate Heart of Mary, I beg of you the conversion of poor sinners.

Aljustrel

Retracing your steps back down the Way of the Cross, you come to the point where you can turn off and walk to Aljustrel, less than a kilometre away. This is where the young seers lived. As you approach this modern, shop-fronted village, try and picture that small, scattered hamlet of a hundred years ago, of about twenty families with their smallholdings, in its bucolic setting, with absolutely no amenities.

You first come across Lucia's house at a road junction: solid, white walled, ancient roof tiles, and clearly marked '*Casa de Lucia*'. You are welcome to enter this humble dwelling of the Santos family, where Lucia lived with her five siblings. You can wander through the few rooms and examine the simple accoutrements, furniture and décor, giving a flavour of family life in Aljustrel in those days. Sr Lucia gave the house to the Sanctuary in 1981.

In the garden at the back, is the well of Arneiro (*Poco do Arneiro*) where the children saw the second apparition of the angel, marked by a statue group of the angel and children. The angel told them to pray very much, and that the Hearts of Jesus and Mary had designs of mercy on them. Here, Jacinta also had a vision of the Holy Father kneeling inside a house, and outside, a crowd throwing stones at him and cursing him.

By the house is a separate, helpful Information Office. Next door to the Santos house is a small museum, showing rural artefacts and agricultural implements of the time.

Not far from the Santos house is that of the Marto family, where Francisco and Jacinta live with their seven siblings. It is similar in style, content and appearance to Lucia's house, and with outside at the rear, a sound example of solid, rustic stone walling and roof tiling at its simplest. In this house Our Lady appeared three times to Jacinta, and once to Francisco and Jacinta. Francisco died here on 4th April 1919.

It is at these houses that you can visualise the simple, hardworking lives of all those in the families who lived here - children as well. For although there was a small school by the church at Fatima, children were required to work the fields and the flocks, and to weave, simply as a necessary contribution to the family livelihoods.

Fatima Parish Church

A kilometre or so from Aljustrel is the church for the parish of Fatima, named after Our Lady of Joys (and also dedicated St Anthony). It was here that the Santos and Marto families worshipped, and where their children received the sacraments.

You approach over a wide, patterned and cobbled parvis, on which, mounted on each side, a statue of Francisco ("Meditate like Francisco") and Jacinta ("Be welcoming

Fatima parish church.

like Jacinta"), and further back, Our Lady. The exterior is white with contrasting red roof tiles, surrounded by olive and palm trees, giving it a very Mediterranean feel.

Inside it appears surprisingly large, with high arches at the sanctuary, transept and along the side naves; a predominantly white interior, contrasting with the dark, solid pews, and above, the dark, panelled, patterned wood ceiling. The font where the seers where baptised is to the left and rear of the church; in the sanctuary the tabernacle is dramatically and effectively illuminated. Francisco spent hours here praying to Our Lord and trying to console him for sins. To the left of the sanctuary is the 'English style' statue of Our Lady of Joys, which was hidden in a wall during the Napoleonic wars, and only rediscovered when the church was being refurbished during the time of the apparitions. On the other side is the statue of Our Lady of the Rosary, which smiled at Lucia and assured her "she would keep my poor heart for God alone", as recorded in her memoirs.

Meditation: *"The World's First Love"*

Mary, then, is for the Muslims the true *Sayyida*, or Lady. The only possible serious rival to her in their creed would be Fatima, the daughter of Mohammed himself. But after the death of Fatima, Mohammed wrote: "Thou shalt be the most blessed of all the women in Paradise, after Mary." In a variant of the text, Fatima is made to say: "I surpass all the women, except Mary."

This brings us to our second point, namely, why the Blessed Mother, in this twentieth century, should have revealed herself in the insignificant little village of Fatima, so that to all future generations she would be known as "Our Lady of Fatima". Since nothing ever happens out of heaven except with a finesse of all details, I believe that the Blessed Virgin chose to be known as "Our Lady of Fatima" as a pledge and a sign of hope to the Muslim people, and as an assurance that they, who show her so much respect, will one day accept her Divine Son, too.
(Archbishop Fulton Sheen)

Prayer: *Prayer for Conversion*

Lord Jesus Christ, most merciful Saviour of the world, we humbly beseech you, by your most Sacred Heart, that all the sheep who stray out of your fold may one day be converted to you, the Shepherd and Bishop of their souls, who lives and reigns with God the Father in the unity of the Holy Spirit, world without end. Amen.

Rosary: *Jesus's Proclamation of the Kingdom of God and the Call to Conversion*
(third decade of the Luminous Mysteries)

The cemetery opposite the church is where the bodies of Francisco and Jacinta lay before being transferred to the Basilica of the Rosary.

Despite its much larger and more prestigious neighbour bearing the name of this village, this parish church is thriving and well attended by its many parishioners.

Back in Fatima

House of Candles

Located with the Postulation Centre for the Canonisation of Blesseds Francisco and Jacinta (Rua de S Pedro), a short walk from the Sanctuary, is this delightful and beautifully presented modern display of Francisco and Jacinta's lives, which includes many family items and artefacts, and with some precious first class relics of these two holy children. A constant visual depiction of those times is displayed, and there is an interactive pictorial display. Here you can sit quietly and meditate about these extraordinary young people and their short, but significant lives. There is also a section devoted to St John Paul II. It is staffed by the Sisters of the Congregation of the Alliance of Holy Mary.

World Apostolate of Fatima

The World Apostolate of Fatima is a Public International Association of the Faithful, approved by the Holy See. It was formed to provide an organisation for Fatima pilgrims and devotees who feel the need keep in touch with Fatima and its spirituality, as well as encourage and affirm each other. Its aims are to promote the authentic teaching of the Catholic Church and its adherence to the tenets of the Gospel; the personal sanctification of its members through faithful observance to the message of Fatima; and, the promotion of the common good by spreading the message of Fatima and encouraging the Fatima devotions. The International Secretariat is directly at the rear and in the grounds of the prominent Domus Pacis Hotel, close to the north east corner of the Sanctuary (off Rua de S Vicente). They welcome visiting pilgrims, and can impart a wealth of knowledge about all that is Fatima. There is a very active branch for England and Wales. Internet addresses of both are at the end of the book.

Museums

There are three museums in Fatima that may be of interest: the Museum of Sacred Art and Ethnology of the Consolata Fathers in Rua Francisco Marto, displaying many sacred objects and items from round the world, reflecting the Consolata's wide mission reach. They also have a chapel, in which you are welcome to pray and reflect. Then there is the Museu Vida da Cristo, also in Rua Francisco Marto, which displays life-size wax figures of many scenes from Christ's life; and lastly, the Museu de Cera (Rua Jacinta Marto), another wax works displaying many varied scenes of life in Portugal at the time of the apparitions, including those of the seers.

Aftermath

Francisco and Jacinta

"I will take Jacinta and Francisco shortly."
(Our Lady in the second apparition)

The influenza epidemic that swept Europe in the autumn of 1918 took the lives of both Francisco and Jacinta. On 3rd April 1919, the day before he died at his home, Francisco made his first Holy Communion, saying to Jacinta, "I am happier than you are, because I have the hidden Jesus in my heart". By his father's account, he died with a smile on his face.

Jacinta suffered prolonged and painful conditions after she contracted the flu, bringing on bronchial pneumonia and an abscess in her chest. Our Lady appeared to her at her home in Aljustrel and asked if she wanted to suffer any more to save sinners. She said she did, and accordingly as Our Lady foretold, she died alone in a Lisbon hospital after unsuccessful surgery to remove two ribs without a general anaesthetic. She succumbed soon after, dying on 20th February 1920, without being able to receive Viaticum.

In 1951, Jacinta's remains were interred in the Basilica at Fatima, and in 1952, they were joined by Francisco's. On 13th May 2000, Pope John Paul II beatified Francisco and

Jacinta in Fatima. The Pope explained that they were being beatified not because of the extraordinary privilege they had in receiving the Blessed Virgin Mary, but because they strove to carry out the requests of Our Lady with utmost fidelity and commitment, displaying and attaining heroic virtue. He described them as "two candles which God lit to illumine humanity in its dark and anxious hours".

The cause for the canonisation of Francisco and Jacinta remains underway, and they will become the first child saints in the history of the Church who died in the ordinary course of family life. Their cause is awaiting any report of a second miracle of healing obtained through their intercession.

Lucia

"...but you will stay here for some time to come."

(Our Lady to Lucia in the second apparition)

After the apparitions, Lucia continued to be the subject of curiosity and constant invasion of her privacy. She did however start her formal education as instructed by Our Lady, eventually giving her the ability to write her marvellous memoirs - *Fatima in Lucia's Own Words*. Because of this harassment, and that her presence at Fatima could be seen to hinder the impartiality of the investigations of the apparitions being undertaken by the Church, she was sent, in 1921, aged fourteen, to the college of the Dorotheans near Oporto. She later joined the Congregation of the Sisters of Saint Dorothy.

During that period she had two more apparitions of Our Lady. The first was in 1925 at the convent in Pontevedra, Spain, of Mary with the Child Jesus. She told Lucia that whoever went to Confession, received Holy Communion, recited five decades of the Rosary, and meditated on the Rosary for fifteen minutes, all with the intention of making reparation to her Immaculate Heart, to be undertaken on the first Saturday of five consecutive months, would receive all the graces necessary for salvation (the devotion of the First Five Saturdays).

The second was in 1929 in the convent chapel at Tuy, also in Spain, when she saw the Holy Trinity, and Christ on the Cross with drops of blood falling over a host suspended above a chalice, and the words, "Grace and Mercy" flowing from the left arm of the cross. Under the right arm of the cross was Mary holding out her Immaculate Heart. She reiterated the statement, made in the July 1917 apparition, that "God asks the Holy Father, in union with all the bishops of the world", to consecrate Russia to her Immaculate Heart.

In 1948 Sr Lucia joined the Carmelite monastery at Coimbra, where she remained for the rest of her long life. She visited Fatima several times, the last being the joyful occasion of the beatification of her cousins, Francisco and Jacinta. She died aged 97 on 13th February 2005. Her remains were interred in the Basilica at Fatima, alongside Jacinta. Her cause for beatification was opened in February

2008 by Pope Benedict XVI, on the third anniversary of her death, thereby waiving the usual five year waiting period.

Approval of the Apparitions

The land at Cova da Iria was gifted to the Church by the Santos family to whom it belonged. Work started on the *Capelinha* in 1919, the first Mass being celebrated there in 1921. On 13th October 1930, after the results of the commission investigating events at Cova da Iria were made known to him, the Bishop of Leiria declared that the apparitions to the shepherd children in the Cova da Iria were "worthy of belief", and that the cult of Our Lady of Fatima could be permitted, the approval thereby sanctioning pilgrimage, and the subsequent development of the Sanctuary.

Portugal

A paper produced by the Center for European Studies, Harvard University, looked at the political effects of Fatima in Portugal following the apparitions. It observed that:

> Throughout…the traditional weakness of Portuguese civil society confirmed the role of the Catholic Church as civil society's dominant institution, and the Catholic community as the wielder of great influence. Fatima has been a major unifying element of that community, [and it concluded that] the reaction of the Catholic faithful to the supposed miraculous events at Fatima is an important and telling element of twentieth century Portuguese life. (Paul Christopher Manuel, "Working Paper No 88").

The grim, stated purpose of the First Republic in 1911 that, "in two generations Catholicism will be completely eliminated in Portugal", clearly failed through the response of the Portuguese faithful to Our Lady of Fatima.

World Events

World events aligning to the prophecies of Fatima would subsequently prove to be the outbreak of World War II - Our Lady specifically naming Pope Pius XI, who was reigning during the Anschluss, when Germany annexed Austria in 1938. And, as graphically depicted in the third apparition: the continuing persecution of the Church over the years, and the attempted assassination of St John Paul II, on the Feast of Our Lady of Fatima, 13th May 1981.

The defining act of Consecration of Russia, abiding by the terms wished for by Our Lady and confirmed by Sr Lucia, was made on 25th March 1984 by Pope John Paul II. In that same month Mikhail Gorbachev was appointed as Head of the Foreign Affairs Committee of the Soviet Union, and a year later became General Secretary of the Communist Party, setting in train over the next three years the events leading to the disbanding of the Warsaw Pact and the eventual dissolution of the USSR. "Everything that happened in Eastern Europe during these last few years would not have been possible without the presence of the Pope," Gorbachev stated in a newspaper article in 1992.

"The power of the Fatima message can convert the communist world."
(Cardinal Yu Pin, Exiled Archbishop of Nanking, 1978)

The Secrets of Fatima

Whilst the seers talked freely about their encounters with Our Lady during the apparitions, they did not divulge the 'three secrets' entrusted to them until in 1941, when Lucia committed to paper the first two parts, at the instruction of the Bishop of Leiria. The first part was the detailed description of their view of hell; the second dealt with devotion to the Immaculate Heart of Mary, and the consecration of Russia to the Immaculate Heart to save souls, and to prevent outbreak of the Second World War.

Two years later the Bishop asked her to record the third part of the secret, which she did in 1944, sealing it in an envelope, asking the Bishop to safeguard it. The envelope, unopened, was passed on to the Secret Archives of the Vatican in 1957.

Successive popes were reported to have read it, but the full text was not officially released until 20th June 2000 by Cardinal Ratzinger, at the direction of Pope John Paul II, soon after the beatification of Jacinta and Francisco. In essence it detailed Our Lady's prophetic warning of wars, persecution of the Church and the suffering of the Holy Father, as described in the July apparition.

As with many episodes involving secrets and mysterious happenings, there tend to be continual rumblings, speculation and conspiracy theories - Fatima is no exception, in this case, with doubts being expressed about full or accurate disclosure. The Church's position was clearly laid out by Cardinal Ratzinger, as Prefect of the Congregation of the Doctrine of Faith, in a detailed commentary on release of the secret on 26th June 2000. The whole fascinating exposé can be read in full by following the Vatican link shown at the back of the book. However, here is the nub:

> And so we come to the final question: What is the meaning of the "secret" of Fatima as a whole (in its three parts)? What does it say to us? First of all we must affirm with Cardinal Sodano: "...the events to which the third part of the 'secret' of Fatima refers now seem part of the past". Insofar as individual events are described, they belong to the past. Those who expected exciting apocalyptic revelations about the end of the world or the future course of history are bound to be disappointed. Fatima does not satisfy our curiosity in this way, just as Christian faith in general cannot be reduced to an object of mere curiosity. What remains was already evident when we began our reflections on the text of the "secret": the exhortation to prayer as the path of "salvation for souls" and, likewise, the summons to penance and conversion.

However, questions were raised again when Pope Benedict XVI on his pilgrimage to the Shrine in May 2010, commented, "We would be mistaken to think that Fatima's prophetic mission is complete".

The Portuguese Cardinal Martins, who accompanied Pope Benedict, gave specific clarification:

> It is important to understand the Pope's words correctly. It is evident that the prophecy of Fatima is not over, and continues to shape the Church and believers. But why? Because the fundamental truths which the Virgin taught in Fatima are extremely relevant and will always be so. They are ever present and sacred values, which cannot be renounced and which are not negotiable.
>
> So Fatima will always have something to say: the content of the message which the Virgin entrusted to the shepherd children and through them, to all men and women of our time. This is why the prophecy is not over, and never will be! (*Inside the Vatican*, June-July 2010)

This makes it clear that some of the historic events attributed to the secrets - World War II, the assassination attempt on Pope John Paul II, and the fall of communism - are over, but, that we can also anticipate other events, including future persecutions of the Church and the Holy Father. But whatever, the compelling appeal of the Fatima message for conversion, prayer, penance and sacrifices for the sins which offend God, will always apply.

"The action of God, the Lord of history, and the co-responsibility of man in the drama of his creative freedom, are the two pillars upon which human history is built.

Our Lady, who appeared at Fatima, recalls these forgotten values. She reminds us that man's future is in God, and that we are active and responsible partners in creating that future."
(Archbishop Tarcisio Bertone, June 2000)

Heading Home

So, as you prepare to head home, you may feel moved to take back with you the messages of Fatima, to ponder and act on them. When looking at what could be involved, this may seem like a 'big ask' in our preoccupied lives. However, big asks do not necessarily have to be answered in a big way, straight away. To start with you could take small, graduated steps. For, in the same way we unswervingly set aside time for our favourite soap or other activity, try also and set aside a time, to ponder, reflect and pray; maybe during that 'dead' period when commuting, or when undertaking some routine repetitive (and boring!) task. And then start gradually unpacking all that you saw and heard and felt at Fatima - particularly the messages of prayer and the Rosary, of sacrifice, reparation and penance - and start putting together some sort of routine - initiating the 'big ask'.

Prayer and the Rosary

"Prayer is an aspiration of the heart, it is a simple glance directed to heaven, it is a cry of gratitude and love in the midst of trial as well as joy; finally, it is something great, supernatural, which expands my soul and unites me to Jesus." (St Therese of Lisieux)

Jesus constantly stressed the importance and efficacy of prayer, and, through the example of his own, constant prayer life. He exhorted perseverance in prayer, and emphasised that, "everything that you ask and pray for, believe that you have it already, and it will be yours" (*Mk* 11:24).

"Pray, pray very much," the angel urged the children, and it was Our Lady who declared: "I am the Lady of the Rosary", and entreated the children to the daily praying of the Rosary: "Continue to pray the Rosary every day to obtain peace for the world and an end to the war". Pope John Paul II, emphasised that, "The Rosary, though clearly Marian in character, is at heart a Christocentric prayer…it has all the depth of the Gospel message in its entirety, of which it can be said to be a compendium".

Yes, a big ask in itself - but try a small step: start by praying just one decade every day, and then maybe once a week committing to any Rosary devotion in your Church (or maybe start one), or pray the Rosary within the family. The devotion of the First Five Saturdays is also a vital part of the big ask, and by Our Lady's gentle request, we should seriously endeavour to comply!

The most sublime sacrifice was the Father offering his Son's life in reparation for all sinners, for all time; and his Son, in his humanity, accepting the will of the Father, consented to an agonising death to consummate that sacrifice. In our own humanity, God also asks us consciously to think about making sacrifices, acts of penance, and acts of reparation - no matter how small or infrequent - for sinners, "especially those in most need of thy mercy". This is such a privilege to know that we can actively contribute to someone's salvation (and our own!) by even a small act offered up.

Please do not be at all put off by these seemingly daunting words 'sacrifice', 'reparation' or 'penance', there is nothing particularly intimidating about all this, because as the Church points out: "The laity…are marvellously called and equipped to produce in all their works, prayers, apostolic endeavours, their ordinary married and family life, their daily labour, their mental and physical relaxation, if carried out in the Spirit, and even the hardships of life, if borne patiently - all of these become spiritual sacrifices acceptable to God through Jesus Christ." (*Lumen Gentium* 34).

It is a simple, but nonetheless unwavering matter of getting in the habit of aligning your thoughts and attitude in offering all these moments as sacrifice, reparation or penance - as well as that daily set aside quiet period with God in prayer; and, in addition, you can send fleeting, ad hoc, but heartfelt 'arrow prayers', having recognised the

moment, and winging them up to God, at any time. Added to all this, is the distinctive value of Eucharistic reparation: joining with the sacrifice of the Mass, receiving Holy Communion, attending holy hours, and visits to the Blessed Sacrament in the tabernacle.

I have made you a light to the nations,
so that my salvation may reach
the remotest parts of the earth. (*Ac* 13:47)

Contacts and Links

Official website of the Shrine of Fatima: *www.fatima.pt/en*

International Secretariat of the World Apostolate of Fatima, in the grounds at the rear of Domus Pacis Hotel (Rua de S Vicente). Visitors welcome: *www.worldfatima.com/*

England and Wales Branch of World Apostolate of Fatima:

www.worldfatima-englandwales.org.uk/

The complete Vatican text on "The Message of Fatima" issued by Cardinal Ratzinger, Prefect of the Congregation for the Doctrine of the Faith, on 26th June: *www.vatican.va/roman_curia/congregations/cfaith/documents/rc_con_cfaith_doc_20000626_message-fatima_en.html*

House of Candles: *www.pastorinhos.com/en/news/house-of-candles-already-open-to-the-public/*

Bibliography

Baldwin, David, *Why Pilgrimage?* (London, Catholic Truth Society, 2015)

Donnelly, Rev Nick, *Loving Mary What Pope Francis Says* (London, Catholic Truth Society, 2016)

Foley, Donal Anthony, *Our Lady and the New Evangelisation* (London, Catholic Truth Society, 2015)

Lucia, Sister Maria, *Fatima in Lucia's Own Words* (Fatima, Portugal, Fundacao Francisco e Jacinta Marto, 2014)

Madigan, Leo, *The Golden Book of Fatima* (Fatima, Portugal, Fatima-Ophel Books, 2007)

Madigan, Leo, *What Happened at Fatima* (London, Catholic Truth Society, 2000)

Nadrah OCist, Fr Anton, *Fatima: Triumph of the Immaculate Heart of Mary Celebrating the Five First Five Saturdays* (London, Catholic Truth Society, 2016)

Tindal-Robertson, Timothy, *Fatima in the Third Millennium* (London, Catholic Truth Society, 2001)

Tindal-Robertson, Timothy, *Message of Fatima* (London, Catholic Truth Society, 1998)

Tindal-Robertson, Timothy, *Fatima, Russia and Pope John Paul II* (Leominster, Gracewing, 1998)

Tindal-Robertson, Timothy and Foley, Donal Anthony, *Fatima's Message and Prayers for Today* (London, Catholic Truth Society, 2016)